CORGI BOOKS

THE GOLDEN RULES OF CRICKET

A CORGI BOOK 0 552 12590 3

First published in Great Britain

PRINTING HISTORY

Corgi edition published 1984

Copyright © Ian Heath 1984

This book is set in 10/11 Souvenir

Corgi Books are published by
Transworld Publishers Ltd.,
Century House, 61-63 Uxbridge Road,
Ealing, London W5 5SA

Made and printed in Great Britain by
Hunt Barnard Printing Ltd., Aylesbury, Bucks.

The Umpires shall satisfy themselves before the start of the match that the wickets are properly pitched.

Any grazing beasts must be removed from the pitch before start of play.

The Umpires shall agree between themselves and inform both Captains before the start of the match on the timepiece to be followed during the match.

The Fieldsman shall ignore any abuse, provocation or interference coming from the spectators.

The Fieldsman may stop the ball with any part of his person, but if he wilfully stops it otherwise, 5 runs shall be added to the run or runs already scored.

The Umpires shall decide whether Bad Light shall stop play.

If a Striker is caught, no runs shall be scored.

The ball is Not Dead when it strikes an Umpire (unless it lodges in his dress).

Before and during a match the Umpires shall ensure that the conduct of the game and the implements used are strictly in accordance with the Laws.

It shall be considered unfair if any Fieldsman wilfully obstructs a Batsman in running.

The Umpires shall stand where they can best see any act upon which their decision may be required.

The Pitch shall not be rolled during a match unless before the start of an innings.

A Runner shall be allowed for a Batsman who during the match is incapacitated by illness or injury.

Only one ball may be used at any one time during a match.

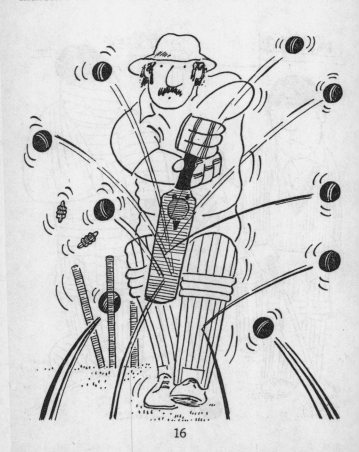

In matches of 2 or more days' duration, the Umpires shall allow, if necessary, the use of quick-setting fillings to repair holes made by the Bowlers and Batsmen.

Sweeping of pitch may be carried out as necessary during the match at the discretion of the Umpires.

Either Umpire shall call and signal 'dead ball' if the ball does not leave the Bowlers hand for any reason.

Any player may appeal to the Umpire.

The Fieldsman should not stand too close to the Striker unless he is adequately protected.

Any form of time wasting is unfair.

In exceptional circumstances, other than those of weather, ground or light, the Umpires may decide to suspend or abandon play.

It is unfair to bowl bouncers at tail-end Batsmen.

If a ball in play cannot be found or recovered any fieldsman may call 'lost ball' when 6 runs shall be added to the score.

All disputes shall be determined by the Umpires and if they disagree the actual state of things shall continue.

The Players shall totally ignore any intruder illegally on the pitch.

The pitch shall not be watered during a match.

The Tea Interval shall be of not more than fifteen minutes duration.

29

Any member of the fielding side may polish the ball provided that such polishing wastes no time and that no artificial substance is used.

For a delivery to be fair the ball must be bowled not thrown.

It is the Players' responsibility to make sure he is adequately protected.

The Umpires shall decide whether rain should stop play.

Before an important match it is advisable for the Player to get as much practise as possible.

During play, the Umpires shall allow either Batsman to beat the pitch with his bat.

The Scorers shall accept and acknowledge all instructions given by the Umpire.

Either Batsman shall be out Obstructing the Field if he wilfully obstructs the opposite side by word or action.

Both Captains shall decide before the match whether drinks may be taken. If so, these intervals shall be one per session and shall not exceed five minutes.

A Batsman shall be considered to have commenced his innings once he has stepped on to the field of play.

The ball, when new, shall weigh not less than 5½ oz (155.9 g), nor more than 5¾ oz (163 g): and shall measure not less than 8¹³⁄₁₆ in (22.4 cm), nor more than 9 in (22.9 cm) in circumference.

If for any reason a Bowler is incapacitated while running up to bowl the first ball of an over, the Umpire shall call and signal 'dead ball'.

If the Bowler bowls the ball so high over or so wide of the wicket that it passes out of reach of the Striker, the Umpire shall call and signal 'wide ball'.

No Fieldsman shall leave the field during play.

Whenever possible the creases shall be re-marked.

The Umpire at the Bowler's end shall stand where he does not interfere with the Bowler's run up.

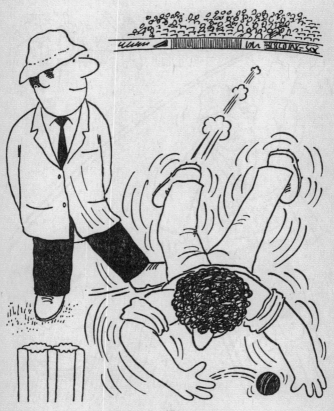

Before the toss of innings two Umpires shall be appointed, one for each end, to control the game with absolute impartiality as required by the Laws.

Discarded clothes must be handed to an Umpire and not left on the pitch.

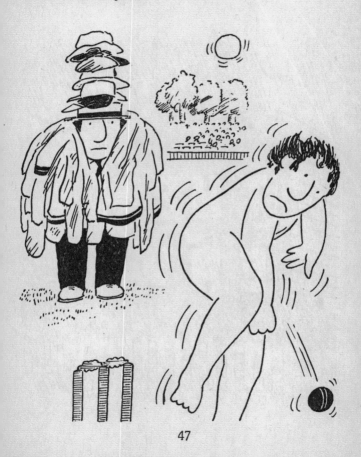